Mental calmness

Challenges involving anxiety & depression and how to overcome it

Marion Drive

All rights been reserved.No part of this publication should be reprinted of transmitted through electronic or mechanical means without prior permission from the author, except for citation for critical uses.

Copyright @ Marion Drive

Table of contents

chapter 1

Figuring out disorders: anxiety and depression

Depression, anxiety, and feelings of anxiety are viewed as significant pointers for emotional well-being, and the powerlessness to identify and address these mental problems adversely influences people.

Depression jumble gives discouraged temperament, loss of interest or joy, diminished energy, sensations of culpability or low self-esteem, upset rest or hunger, unfortunate fixation, issue of reasoning and simply deciding, and, in extreme stages, repeating contemplations of death or self destruction. Among the psychological problems, depression is an infection of worldwide weight influencing 350 million individuals around the world.

Anxiety is a reaction of the body to an apparent danger which is set off by a singular's convictions, sentiments, and considerations and is described by stressing contemplations, strain, expanded pulse, respiratory rate, and heartbeat rate, perspiring, tipsiness, chest torment, and trouble of gulping. Anxiety issues are the most common mental problems with an ongoing overall predominance of 7.3%.

Stress is viewed as a physiological response of a living being where various protection instrument becomes possibly the most important factor to defy what is happening which is seen as compromising or expanded request. It is likewise notable that pressure is a huge gamble factor for the improvement of illicit drug use and compulsion backslide. Notwithstanding being a laid out training, the possible dangers and advantages of khat biting are extremely controversial, especially with respect to the relationship among khat and psychological maladjustment. There are many case provides details regarding a potential relationship between unnecessary khat use and the event of mental problems, like hyper like psychosis and the occurrence of maniacal side effects. Concentrates on called attention to that incessant khat clients showed anxiety, depression, and stress, more over and again than khat chewers. Those mental issues of khat biting are firmly connected with the seriousness of reliance scale (SDS) on khat. "The heavier and more incessant the utilization, the more prominent the gamble supposedly was" Substance misuse and related issues are of flow worldwide worry that prompts emotional wellness problems which contributed around 14% of the worldwide weight of the sickness. It has turned into a pandemic in certain pieces of the African area with youths being the primary casualties of the chronic sickness and social impacts of substance use. Substance misuse, including khat biting, is just about as old as the historical backdrop of humanity .

Anxiety problems are genuine, serious ailments - similarly as genuine and serious as actual issues like coronary illness or diabetes. Anxiety problems are the most widely recognized and unavoidable mental issues in the US.

Depression is a condition where an individual feels deterred, miserable, irredeemable, unmotivated, or uninvolved in life overall for over about fourteen days and when the sentiments obstruct day to day exercises.

Significant depression is a treatable disease that influences the manner in which an individual thinks, feels, acts, and works. Anytime, 3 to 5 percent of individuals experience the ill effects of significant depression; the lifetime risk is around 17%.

It's a typical piece of life to encounter periodic anxiety.

Yet, you might encounter anxiety that is determined, apparently wild, and overpowering. Assuming it's an unnecessary, unreasonable fear of regular circumstances, it tends to debilitate. At the point when anxiety slows down everyday exercises issue.

The expression "anxiety jumble" alludes to explicit mental issues that include intense trepidation or stress, and incorporates summed up anxiety jumble (Stray), alarm confusion and fits of anxiety, agoraphobia, social anxiety problem, particular mutism, fear of abandonment, and explicit fears.
Fanatical enthusiastic problem (OCD) and post-awful pressure issue (PTSD) are firmly

connected with anxiety issues, which some might insight simultaneously as depression.

"It's a cycle," "When you get restless, you will quite often have this unavoidable pondering some concern or some issue. You regret it. Then you feel like you've fizzled. You move to depression."

These two issues - anxiety and depression - have a confounded relationship:

The possibility gaining depression is a lot higher when an anxiety problem as of now exists. Almost 50% of those with significant depression additionally experience the ill effects of extreme and industrious anxiety.
Individuals who are discouraged frequently feel restless and stressed. One can undoubtedly set off the other, with anxiety frequently going before depression.
Individuals with post-horrible pressure problem (PTSD) are particularly inclined to creating depression.
An organic inclination for both of these circumstances if frequently at the foundation of

a singular's fight. This is by all accounts valid with anxiety problems much more than with depression. Connolly makes sense of, "Certain individuals are simply worriers and pass it down."

Individuals with an anxiety issue ought to talk with a specialist, specialist or other medical services proficient about their side effects. Treatment for an anxiety issue ought not be postponed. In the event that not trapped in time, depression might find the entryway completely open for moving in and setting up house in those people.

Chapter 2
Causes for anxiety and depression

Family background of emotional wellness conditions

Certain individuals who experience anxiety conditions might have a hereditary inclination towards anxiety and these circumstances can once in a while run in a family. Nonetheless, having a parent or direct relation experience anxiety or other emotional well-being condition doesn't mean you'll naturally foster anxiety.

Character factors

Research proposes that individuals with specific character qualities are bound to have anxiety. For instance, youngsters who are sticklers, effortlessly bothered, bashful, hindered, need confidence or need to control everything, once in a while foster anxiety during youth, pre-adulthood or as grown-ups.

Progressing unpleasant occasions

Anxiety conditions might create as a result of at least one upsetting life altering situations. Normal triggers include:

work pressure or occupation change
change in living game plans
pregnancy and conceiving an offspring
family and relationship issues
major profound shock following an upsetting or horrendous mishap
verbal, sexual, physical or psychological mistreatment or injury
passing or loss of a friend or family member.

Actual medical conditions

Constant actual sickness can likewise add to anxiety conditions or effect on the therapy of either the anxiety or the actual disease itself. Normal persistent circumstances related with anxiety conditions include:

diabetes
asthma
hypertension and coronary illness

A few states of being can mirror anxiety conditions, similar to an overactive thyroid. It very well may be valuable to see a specialist and be surveyed to decide if there might be a clinical reason for your sensations of anxiety.

Other emotional wellness conditions

While certain individuals might encounter an anxiety condition all alone, others might encounter different anxiety conditions, or other psychological wellness conditions. Depression and anxiety conditions frequently happen together. It means quite a bit to check for and get help for this large number of conditions simultaneously.

Substance use

Certain individuals who experience anxiety might utilize liquor or different medications to assist them with dealing with their condition. At times, this might prompt individuals fostering a substance use issue alongside their anxiety condition. Liquor and substance use can irritate anxiety conditions especially as the impacts of the substance wear off. It means a lot to check for and get help for any substance use conditions simultaneously.

I recommend that depression is a political peculiarity to the extent that it has political sources and results. I then examine one part of this contention — whether depression diminishes cooperation. I estimate that people with depression come up short on inspiration and actual ability to cast a ballot and participate in different types of political support because of physical issues and sensations of sadness and unresponsiveness. In addition, I analyze how depression in pre-adulthood can have downstream ramifications for cooperation in youthful adulthood. The investigations, utilizing both cross-sectional and longitudinal information, show that elector turnout and different types of interest decline as the seriousness of discouraged state of mind increments. These discoveries are examined considering incapacity privileges and likely endeavors to support interest among this gathering.

Recall ...
Everybody's unique and it's generally expected a mix of elements that can add to fostering an anxiety condition. It's memorable's essential that you can't necessarily distinguish the reason for anxiety or change troublesome conditions. The main thing is to perceive the signs and side effects and look for counsel and backing.

Chapter 3
Types and side effects of anxiety and depression

Summed up Anxiety Problem

Summed up Anxiety Problem, Stray, is an anxiety problem described by constant anxiety, overstated stress, and pressure, in any event, when nothing remains to be incited.

Fanatical Impulsive Issue (OCD)

Fanatical Impulsive Problem, OCD, is an anxiety issue and is described by intermittent, undesirable contemplations (fixations) as well as tedious ways of behaving (impulses). Monotonous ways of behaving, for example, hand washing, counting, checking, or cleaning are frequently performed with the expectation of forestalling over-the-top contemplations or making them disappear. Playing out these alleged "ceremonies," be that as it may, gives just impermanent alleviation, and not performing them particularly increments anxiety.

Alarm Confusion

An alarm jumble is an anxiety problem and is described by unforeseen and rehashed episodes of extraordinary apprehension joined by actual side effects that might incorporate chest torment, heart palpitations, windedness, wooziness, or stomach trouble.

Post-Horrendous Pressure Issue (PTSD)
Post-Horrendous Pressure Problem, PTSD, is an anxiety issue that can foster after openness to a frightening occasion or difficulty in which grave actual damage happened or was undermined. Horrible mishaps that might set off PTSD incorporate vicious individual attacks, regular or human-caused catastrophes, mishaps, or military battles.

Social Fear (or Social Anxiety Issue)
Social Fear, or Social Anxiety Problem, is an anxiety issue described as overpowering anxiety and unreasonable hesitance in regular social circumstances. Social fear can be restricted to just a single kind of circumstance - like anxiety toward talking in formal or casual circumstances, or eating or drinking before others - or, in its most extreme structure, might

be expansive to the point that an individual encounters side effects nearly whenever they are around others.

Agoraphobia. You have an extreme feeling of dread toward being where it appears hard to get away or find support if a crisis happens. For instance, you might frenzy or feel restless when on a plane, on public transportation, or while remaining following a group.

Specific mutism. This is a sort of friendly anxiety wherein small children who talk typically with their family don't talk in that frame of mind, at school.

Medicine incited anxiety jumble. Utilization of specific prescriptions or unlawful medications, or withdrawal from specific medications, can set off certain side effects of anxiety problems.

Fear of abandonment. Young children aren't the ones in particular who feel frightened or restless when a friend or family member leaves. Anybody can get fear abandonment. If you do, you'll feel exceptionally restless or unfortunate when an individual you're close with leaves your sight. You'll continuously stress that something terrible may happen to your adored one.

Anxiety Turmoil Side effects

The fundamental side effect of anxiety problems is inordinate apprehension or stress. Anxiety problems can likewise make it hard to inhale, rest, remain still, and concentrate. Your particular side effects rely upon the sort of anxiety problem you have.

Normal side effects are:

Frenzy, dread, and disquiet

Sensations of frenzy, destruction, or risk

Rest issues

Not having the option to keep even-tempered yet

Cold, sweat-soaked, numb, or shivering hands or feet

Windedness

Breathing quicker and more rapidly than ordinary (hyperventilation)

Heart palpitations

Dry mouth

Queasiness

Tense muscles
Unsteadiness
Pondering an issue again and again and unfit to stop (rumination)
Powerlessness to focus
Seriously or fanatically staying away from dreaded items or spots

Chapter 4
Challenges involving this disorders

Everyday issues influence significant parts of your life, similar to connections and work, can immensely affect your emotional wellness. At the point when they don't disappear, or get greater, the feelings they cause can overpower you and can be an exceptionally large test to them.

Continuous difficulties in significant areas of day to day existence, similar to marriage, whānau and work, can immensely affect your emotional well-being. It deteriorates when one issue begins prompting others.
Many individuals face a scope of dependable issues, conflicts and dangers in their regular routines. These can incorporate issues with individuals near us like an accomplice or youngsters; love or sex issues; progressing disease or incapacity; or issues with work (mahi) or school (kura). These issues might come on top of difficulties you've had to deal with before throughout everyday life.

It's particularly intense assuming that those previous difficulties were never settled despite everything make you respond emphatically. The consequences of this pressure can appear in any or all region of our prosperity. Various things can add to it, for instance:

not having the option to accomplish your objectives
being baffled by what's generally anticipated of you
cash issues
actual inability
persistent ailment
progressing hardships with individuals in your day to day existence.

Cash issues
It is distressing to Live on a low pay. It can hugely affect confidence and leave you feeling as though you're letting individuals down, particularly as your whānau develops. Attempting to accommodate your whānau's necessities while overseeing obligation can be troublesome. Discussing what is happening

with everybody, even the kids or mokopuna, can assist them with understanding the reason why they can't have all that they request. Assuming command of the things you can change will assist you with remaining positive and associated with whānau and companions.
It can help in the event that you:
financial plan so you take advantage of the cash you have
put forth yourself objectives
give yourself an opportunity to thoroughly consider choices
track down free activities
invest energy spending time with your kids or mokopuna.
In the event that things are getting truly extreme and you can't bear the cost of the fundamentals, make it a point to for more assistance:

www.birthright.org.nz Data and backing for single parent whānau.
www.workandincome.govt.nz Data about monetary help and business administrations.
www.familybudgeting.org.nz New Zealand Alliance of Family Planning Administrations Inc.

www.hnzc.co.nz Lodging New Zealand.
www.sorted.org.nz Autonomous Cash Guide.

Separation
Separation is the point at which you're judged and treated unjustifiably or inadequately on account of the gathering you have a place with, instead of on what your identity is.

Bunches that can be victimized incorporate individuals with experience of depression or anxiety, individuals whose nationality, culture, orientation personality or sexual direction is unique in relation to that of the vast majority around them, individuals who are handicapped and more seasoned individuals.

In the event that you're not piece of the standard culture, this segregation can be a reason for trouble. You might try and begin to put stock in what others are talking about freely. This can then bring about you:

liking to be separated from everyone else
feeling baffled
flying off the handle

not putting stock in yourself
losing trust in your capacities
not going for occupations
not proceeding with your schooling
passing up getting things done in life you truly needed to do.
Assuming you're oppressed in light of psychological maladjustment, the subsequent sentiments and the manner in which you see yourself might keep you from looking for help. That implies you pass up the treatment and support that can assist you with recuperating. The Like Personalities, Similar to Mine program has important data about segregation. It gives a rundown of spots you can find support from in the event that you feel you're being victimized.

Handicap is extremely normal. One out of four New Zealanders lives with an inability.

Having an actual debilitation, scholarly or learning inability doesn't naturally imply that your psychological prosperity will be impacted. Yet, certain individuals with handicaps experience difficulties and hardships that can prompt pressure and avoidance from the more extensive local area.

A handicap can cause sentiments that influence your emotional well-being. You could insight:

sensations of melancholy and misfortune
disappointment
frustration at not having the option to arrive at life objectives
a deficiency of character in the event that the handicap came to fruition in adulthood.
It's truly vital to tell others what difficulties you're confronting and the way that you're feeling.

Numerous others living with a handicap share your dissatisfaction of facing a daily reality such that hasn't considered their remarkable necessities and that doesn't perceive their assets. Chatting with them can be an incredible spot to begin.

Don't hesitate for even a moment to request proficient assistance as you deal with the progressions to your life.

There are numerous organizations and social developments that give data and backing to individuals with inabilities. The following are a couple:

http://www.dpa.org.nz (DPA) is a Debilitated Individual's Association (DPO) that incorporates all incapacity gatherings. It centers around accomplishing consideration for every New Zealander.
www.health.govt.nz/our-work/inability administrations Service of Wellbeing data about administrations to help individuals with handicaps.
www.workandincome.govt.nz/qualification/wellbeing and-inability/index.html Data about monetary help and work administrations.
www.beaccessible.org.nz Data on open conditions.
workbridge.co.nz An expert business administration for individuals with a wide range of handicap, injury or sickness.

Liquor and different medications

While liquor and different medications can emphatically affect our mind-set, in the more extended term they don't help, and are connected to a scope of psychological wellness issues.
You might drink liquor to assist you with unwinding, lift your temperament, feel less restless in friendly circumstances, get to rest, or to conceal different issues. However, when taken in bigger sums, liquor is a depressant and will really exacerbate you. The eventual outcomes of an excess of liquor generally exacerbate anxiety. Drinking can likewise influence your associations with accomplices, whānau and companions, and effect on your work. The equivalent is valid for different medications like weed and methamphetamine. Liquor can change the impacts of doctor prescribed medications or different medications and can exacerbate their secondary effects. It can likewise make depression and anxiety harder to analyze or treat.

assuming you're stressed over your drinking , converse with your primary care physician or another wellbeing proficient. You can likewise call the Liquor Medication Helpline free of charge on 0800 787 797 or free text 8681.

Alcohol.org.nz has loads of data and apparatuses to assist you with finding out about what liquor means for you, or how much liquor is in what you drink. It additionally has the Is Your Drinking Alright? test you can take on the off chance that you keep thinking about whether your drinking may be an issue. In the event that you're stressed over drugs, you can beware of your medication stepping through propensities with the Exam Your Medication Taking apparatus from the Liquor Medication Helpline site.

Long haul Ailments

Many individuals live with long haul ailments. As far as some might be concerned, this littly affects their life and the side effects are overseen without any problem. For other people, everyday living can be truly troublesome.

A few long haul conditions can straightforwardly influence your emotional wellness (for instance diabetes, stroke, and thyroid issues). In any case, for the vast majority individuals the challenges can show up with living with a drawn out condition that add to depression or anxiety. These challenges include:

constant agony
head wounds
sorrow that you have lost your feeling of yourself as a sound individual
decreased pay
the results of drug or treatment
loss of social help
losing your autonomy
stressing over others expecting to really focus on you
not having the option to do things you used to appreciate.

Specialists and other wellbeing experts are turning out to be more mindful that having a drawn out condition can influence your psychological well-being. Nonetheless, they are probably going to be most worried about your actual wellbeing. You really must share any worries you have about your feelings or emotional well-being.

Being know all about the signs and side effects of depression and anxiety yourself is vital. Consider any irrelevant actual aggravation, outrageous sleepiness, loss of focus, sensations of sadness or anxiety about your wellbeing.

Chapter 5
Instructions to defeat anxiety and depression

You've seen a few changes recently. Perhaps you feel miserable, sad, or get no bliss out of exercises that used to be entertaining. Seems like depression, acceptable?

Perhaps that is not all. In some cases you're concerned, apprehensive, and downright uncomfortable. Isn't that an indication of anxiety?

Not all that quick. It's generally expected to have promising and less promising times or to have things you're worried about. You may be going through a troublesome time. Your primary care physician can assist you with sorting out whether or not it's really a condition and what might help.

Depression and anxiety resemble flip sides of a similar coin, "Being discouraged frequently makes us restless, and anxiety frequently makes us discouraged."

In the event that you have the two circumstances, there are heaps of ways of finding support.

Talk Treatment (Guiding)

An expert specialist can foster an arrangement to treat your anxiety and depression simultaneously.

A few kinds of treatment that can help are:

Mental social treatment. It helps you to change your contemplations and activities.

Relational treatment. It tells you the best way to convey better.

Critical thinking treatment. It gives you abilities to deal with your side effects.

You can find a specialist who spends significant time in these through the Anxiety Problems Relationship of America. Or on the other hand ask your PCP for a reference.

Drug

Your PCP might recommend an upper medication that treats both depression and anxiety side effects, like a SSRI (specific serotonin reuptake inhibitor), a SNRI (serotonin-norepinephrine reuptake inhibitor), or others like bupropion and mirtazapine.

A few instances of SSRIs are:
Citalopram (Celexa)
Escitalopram (Lexapro)
Fluoxetine (Prozac, Sarafem, Symbyax)
Fluvoxamine (Luvox)
Paroxetine (Paxil)
Sertraline (Zoloft)
Vilazodone (Viibryd)

A few instances of SNRIs are:
Desvenlafaxine (Khedezla, Pristiq)
Duloxetine (Cymbalta)
Levomilnacipran (Fetzima)
Venlafaxine (Effexor)

Instances of bupropion include:
Aplenzin
Wellbutrin
Wellbutrin SR
Wellbutrin XL
Educate your PCP regarding every one of your side effects so they can conclude which is ideal. Likewise notice any enhancements you

take, regardless of whether they are normal, on the off chance that they could influence your treatment.

It might require half a month or months for your medication to work. You might need to attempt a couple sorts before you find one that is best for you.

Work out

It's a demonstrated state of mind supporter that is great for your body and psyche. Practice likewise raises your confidence and certainty and can work on your connections.

Furthermore, it's viewed as a treatment for gentle to direct depression.

"Indeed, even a lively walk can kick off the endorphins," which are synthetic substances in your cerebrum that assist you with feeling much better.

High-energy and regular work-out is ideal. Intend to do it something like 3-5 times each week. In the event that you really want inspiration, go with companions or join a gathering.

Unwinding Procedures
Give yoga, reflection, and breathing activities an attempt.
Thinking for only 2-5 minutes during the day can facilitate your anxiety and ease up your state of mind.
Center around your breath.
Make an image to you of a lovely picture.
Rehash a straightforward word or mantra, similar to "love" or "joy."

Really take a look at Your Eating routine
Try not to let solace food put your dietary patterns out of equilibrium. Anxiety and depression frequently trigger desires for carbs. Pick lean protein with a tad of sound fats to feel more fulfilled and more settled. Furthermore, fill a portion of your plate with products of the soil. Limit or stay away from sugar, caffeine, and liquor.

Get Backing
Solid connections assist you with feeling improved. Connect with loved ones and let them in on the thing you're going through so they support you.

You can likewise join a care group, where you'll meet individuals who are going through a portion of exactly the same things you are.

Make A few Strides all alone
Get coordinated. "Less mess in your actual environmental factors, email inbox, and to-do container will assist your brain with being more at ease,".You don't need to handle everything simultaneously. Make an arrangement to deal with each area in turn.

Make new objectives. Is there something you've for practically forever needed to do, or a spot you need to go? Make a bit by bit, reasonable arrangement to get it going.

Accomplish something significant. Engage in a movement that feels essential to you. It could be athletic, political, otherworldly, or a social reason where you can chip in. Search for something that provides you a feeling of motivation.

Be innovative. Direct your concentration into something productive. Rediscover your assets.

On the off chance that you have a tragically missing ability or interest, jump once again into it. Braslow proposes attempting verse, music, photography, or plan.

Peruse a decent book. It's an incredible method for unwinding. There's even exploration that shows that perusing books on otherworldliness or brain research might help your state of mind.

www.ingramcontent.com/pod-product-compliance
Lightning Source LLC
LaVergne TN
LVHW020536160826
845677LV00015B/4081

* 9 7 9 8 8 4 5 8 4 7 3 2 4 *